唐可儿奇遇记

PRINCE MUD-TURTLE

解救泥龟王子

【美】莱曼·弗兰克·鲍姆 著

【美】梅金尼尔·恩赖特 绘

马爱农 译　　晓 华 + Emma 朗读

中国国际广播出版社

让优秀的双语桥梁书引领孩子进入英语文学世界（代序）

晓华

《唐可儿奇遇记》是美国儿童文学家弗兰克·鲍姆（L. Frank Baum）所著的另一隐秘的奇幻佳作，风靡西方百年后，首次在中国面世。作为《绿野仙踪》的作者，鲍姆在中国可算是大名鼎鼎，但知道或读过《唐可儿奇遇记》的人却并不多。

弗兰克·鲍姆是位极为高产的作家。他一生写过六十二本书，大多数都是为孩子写的，其中光是由《绿野仙踪》的故事延伸出来的奥兹国系列小说就有十四本，此外还有不少书，其中的人物多与奥兹国有关。

《唐可儿奇遇记》是一个完全独立的童话故事系列，以生活在草原小镇上的小姑娘唐可儿为主角，讲述了她在动物世界的神奇冒险。与《绿野仙踪》中的多萝西一样，唐可儿活泼大胆、心直口快，并且，据说这两个人物的原型，其实是同一个人，都是鲍姆妻子的外甥女玛格达雷娜。玛格达雷娜一家住在达科他草原的埃奇利小镇上，鲍姆笔下的唐可儿也住在埃奇利小镇。而多萝西的家乡虽然在堪萨斯，可《绿野仙踪》中描写的她家周围的环境，与达科他草原其实并无二致。

　　有意思的是，在《唐可儿奇遇记》首次出版时，鲍姆并没有署自己的名字，而是使用了笔名 Laura Bancroft。鲍姆的大量作品都使用了不同的笔名，有人说这是因为他太能写了，用笔名是不想市面上同时出现太多部他写的书，互相之间形成竞争。不过，也许是因为这套小说出版之后卖得太好，又或许是鲍姆认为这一系列和《绿野仙踪》一样都是自己的得意之作，到《唐可儿奇遇记》再版的时候，他就又署回了本名，弗兰克·鲍姆。

《唐可儿奇遇记》系列包括六本小说，此次中国国际广播出版社带给读者的是其中的三本。《唐可儿梦游仙境》主要讲述了唐可儿去大峡谷采蓝莓，她不听甲壳虫的警告，越过了那条魔法线，遇到了能说会动的石头；喜欢吃奶油的蝴蝶；跑得飞快的书本以及故弄玄虚的黄鼠狼等奇妙的现象，并受邀参加舞会的故事。《糖块山》中的故事，则是在潜移默化中帮助孩子了解社会层次，两个孩子无意中进入神秘的城市，在其中遇上各色人群，应付审问和意外，还见证假冒的贵族如何身份败露以及焦虑的公主如何保住地位。《解救泥龟王子》的故事梗概是，唐可儿在小溪边玩耍时抓住了一只会说话的泥龟，经过一番冒险之后，帮助它变回了仙境王子。

　　《唐可儿奇遇记》中的故事传达出的，是人和动物间相互尊重、和谐相处的讯息。比如，在《土拨鼠先生》中，鲍姆借着土拨鼠先生之口，说出了这样一段话："你们残忍地对待可怜的动物，而他们不过是别无他法，找不到吃的就得饿死。其实广阔的田野上生长的东西足够人类和我们都吃的。"

在鲍姆看来，人类按照自己的利益划分动物好坏，进而铲除"坏动物"的行为，实在是一种残忍。

　　青蛙吃蚊子，所以需要保护；蝗虫吃庄稼，于是需要消灭。在大人们的世界里，按照自己的利益来划分动物是有益还是有害并没有什么不妥。可孩子们不一定这样看。他们对自然世界的尊重，似乎已经超越了我们。前几天，我和女儿Emma在小区散步时，发现一只长尾长身的鼠族动物在马路上一蹿而过。我心里一阵硌硬，正想把过街老鼠的成语解释给她听，她却嚷道："啊！好可爱的大老鼠！"说得我无言以对。也许，像《唐可儿奇遇记》这样以自然和动物为题材的童话故事，之所以受到孩子们的喜爱，正是因为这些故事跳出了一般大人们那狭隘的善恶观吧。

　　《唐可儿奇遇记》系列是鲍姆专为年龄较小的读者写的章节书，文字上比《绿野仙踪》更简单，也更短小精悍，适合八岁以上、英语水平较好的孩子独立阅读。从亲子阅读到独立阅读，是一个了不起的跨越，也是养成阅读兴趣和习惯的关键期。孩子从依偎在父母身边聆听、翻看绘本，到独自探索英文文字的世界，这期间，寻找到合适的阅读内容对他们至关重要。专门为大孩子而写的章节书，可以说是一个完美的过渡。章节书在词汇、句子长度和内容方面都照顾到年轻读者的需求，篇幅比绘本长了许多，插图减少了，但是故事分成了一个个短章节，一天看不完没关系，夹上书签，把书放在枕边，第二天接着看就好了。

我特别遗憾自己在少年时期没能接触到这样的章节书。在原版英文读物并不丰富的年代，我的英文阅读之旅，从《新概念英语》开始，一下就蹦到了《简爱》《荆棘鸟》之类的经典小说。这些大部头不光生词多，深刻程度也超出我的理解范围，导致我不得不跳过大段大段的描写。直到现在我看原版小说还有个坏习惯，就是看不大进去风景描写，一味贪图情节发展。章节书，对于循序渐进的阅读，对于培养良好的阅读习惯，真是太重要了。

《唐可儿奇遇记》系列的英文版每个故事大约四五千字，分为八个章节，也就是说每一章只有七百个字左右，再加上每本书都配有十几张精美的彩页插图，孩子们读起来一定不会觉得累。书的排版上也充分照顾到孩子们，中英双语分段排版，遇到不认识的字词可以迅速查到中文。如果读得累了，还可以听一听我和女儿 Emma 录制的双语朗读版，用耳朵享受大师的经典之作。其实听书，也是一种重要的语言学习方式。不管孩子还是大人，在阅读有一定难度的文字时，是不是都特别希望有人能读给自己听？这是因为，听书时眼睛得到了解放，并且，优美的朗读，可以使人更容易进入到文字描绘出的情境中去。

　　在各类儿童英文读物已经很丰富的当下，为孩子选择经典佳作显得尤为重要。一套好的作品，会引领孩子进入英语文学的殿堂。而好书不会被时间埋没。我相信，弗兰克·鲍姆的这套《唐可儿奇遇记》，一百年后仍然会焕发光彩，受到中国孩子们的喜爱。

目录
List of Chapters

唐可儿
抓住了乌龟

Twinkle
Captures the Turtle

在一个炎热的夏天，唐可儿顺着草坡走下去，来到小溪边。溪水要么唱着歌儿在石头上流过，要么奔腾向前，绕过弯弯曲曲的溪岸，懒洋洋地在较为宽阔的浅水区流淌。说实在的，它不能算一条小溪，因为许多地方那么窄，一个敏捷的小孩子一跳就能跳过去。可是方圆好几英里内，这是唯一的一条小溪。对唐可儿来说，它简直是一个永不枯竭的快乐的源泉。

ONE hot summer day Twinkle went down into the meadow to where the brook ran tinkling over its stones or rushed and whirled around the curves of the banks or floated lazily through the more wide and shallow parts. It wasn't much of a brook, to tell the facts, for there were many places where an active child could leap across it. But it was the only brook for miles around, and to Twinkle it was a never-ending source of delight.

蹚水踩在布满鹅卵石的水底，让微微的涟漪轻轻拂过纤细的脚踝，还有什么比这更能让小姑娘开心和欢畅的呢？

在牧场南面的一处地方，溪水较深，里面有真正的鱼儿游来游去，比如"尖角大王""白鲑""小亮灯"。偶尔，还能在青石板边缘的底下，在岸边的小洞洞里抓到一只泥龟（泥龟：乌龟的别称）呢。

Nothing amused or refreshed the little girl more than to go wading on the pebbly bottom and let the little waves wash around her slim ankles.

There was one place, just below the pasture lot, where it was deeper; and here there were real fishes swimming about, such as "horned aces" and "chubs" and "shiners"; and once in a while you could catch a mud-turtle under the edges of the flat stones or in hollows beneath the banks.

深水区不大，只是一个水洼，但唐可儿从来不敢在里面蹚水，因为水会齐到她的腰，肯定会把她的裙子打湿，惹来妈妈的好一顿数落。

今天，唐可儿翻过小路上的栅栏，那儿正好有座摇摇晃晃的木桥横跨小溪。她一屁股坐在溪岸的草坡上，脱掉了鞋袜。然后，她戴上太阳帽，不让太阳晒到自己的脸，轻轻地走进小溪，站在那里，注视着清凉的溪水在腿边流过。

The deep part was not very big, being merely a pool, but Twinkle never waded in it, because the water would come quite up to her waist, and then she would be sure to get her skirts wet, which would mean a good scolding from mamma.

To-day she climbed the fence in the lane, just where the rickety wooden bridge crossed the brook, and at once sat down upon the grassy bank and took off her shoes and stockings. Then, wearing her sun-bonnet to shield her face from the sun, she stepped softly into the brook and stood watching the cool water rush by her legs.

唐可儿准备蹚水

Twinkle Prepares to Go Wading

这感觉非常舒服和愉快，可是一动不动地站着，唐可儿坚持不了很长时间。于是，她开始慢慢地蹚水往下游走，一直走在小溪中间，透过清亮的溪水寻找最适合落脚的地方。

　　不一会儿，她不得不低下脑袋，钻过把草坡和牧场隔开的那道栅栏。总算顺利地钻过来了，她继续往下游走，最后来到深水洼的旁边。

It was very nice and pleasant; but Twinkle never could stand still for very long, so she began to wade slowly down the stream, keeping in the middle of the brook, and being able to see through the clear water all the best places to put her feet.

Pretty soon she had to duck her head to pass under the fence that separated the meadow from the pasture lot; but she got through all right, and then kept on down the stream, until she came close to the deep pool.

我刚才已经说了，唐可儿不能蹚过深水洼。于是，她来到岸上，然后跪下来，悄没声儿地爬到岸边。这样，如果有鱼儿在水洼里游动，就不会被她吓跑了。

　　She couldn't wade through this, as I have explained; so she got on dry land and crept on her hands and knees up to the edge of the bank, so as not to scare the fishes, if any were swimming in the pool.

运气真不错，今天水洼里有好几条鱼呢，它们似乎根本没注意到唐可儿在看它们，因为唐可儿的动作这么轻。有一条小鱼的身体滑溜溜的，被阳光一照，像银子一样发亮。小姑娘看着它一扭一扭地游过来游过去，感到开心极了。还有一条颜色跟泥巴一样的大鱼，沉在水底，好长时间不动弹，只是鱼鳍和尾巴尖儿偶尔动一动。唐可儿还发现一个小鱼群，由几条最多一寸长的小鱼组成，总是聚在一起游动，就像一家人似的。

By good luck there were several fishes in the pool to-day, and they didn't seem to notice that Twinkle was looking at them, so quiet had she been. One little fellow shone like silver when the sunshine caught his glossy sides, and the little girl watched him wiggling here and there with much delight. There was also a big, mud-colored fish that lay a long time upon the bottom without moving anything except his fins and the tip of his tail, and Twinkle also discovered a group of several small fishes not over an inch long, that always swam together in a bunch, as if they belonged to one family.

唐可儿抓住了乌龟

Twinkle Captures the Turtle

小姑娘热切地注视着这些小动物，看了很长时间。对于这些普普通通的鱼儿，水洼就是它们所知道的整个世界。它们在这里出生，也在这里死去，永远不会离开这个地方，甚至不知道外面还有一个比这大得多的世界。

The girl watched these little creatures long and earnestly. The pool was all of the world these simple fishes would ever know. They were born here, and would die here, without ever getting away from the place, or even knowing there was a much bigger world outside of it.

过了一阵儿，小姑娘注意到，在她躺着的岸边，溪水变得有点儿混浊。当水面慢慢地重新变得清澈时，她看见一只美丽的乌龟，就趴在她的脑袋下面，紧贴着溪岸。

　　乌龟比一枚银币稍微大一点点，龟壳虽然是一种灰暗的褐色，跟唐可儿见过的其他泥龟没有什么两样，但是这只乌龟的背部有着一块块鲜艳的黄色和红色的斑块。

After a time the child noticed that the water had become a little muddy near the edge of the bank where she lay, and as it slowly grew clear again she saw a beautiful turtle lying just under her head and against the side of the bank.

It was a little bigger around than a silver dollar, and instead of its shell being of a dull brown color, like that of all other mud-turtles she had seen, this one's back was streaked with brilliant patches of yellow and red.

"我必须抓住这只可爱的乌龟！"唐可儿想。乌龟趴的地方水比较浅，唐可儿突然把手伸进去，一把抓住了乌龟，迅速把它捞出来扔在了岸上。乌龟肚皮朝天躺在那儿，拼命地摆动四条胖乎乎的腿，想把身体翻过来。

"I must get that lovely turtle!" thought Twinkle; and as the water was shallow where it lay she suddenly plunged in her hand, grabbed the turtle, and flung it out of the water on to the bank, where it fell upon its back, wiggling its four fat legs desperately in an attempt to turn over.

第二章
Chapter II

唐可儿发现
乌龟会说话
Twinkle Discovers
the Turtle Can Talk

水里突然这么一阵骚动，鱼儿们吓得四散逃开，一眨眼就没影儿了。可是唐可儿并不在意，她现在的兴趣都集中在那只挣扎的乌龟身上了。

她跪在草地上，俯身打量着乌龟。就在这时，她仿佛听见一个小声音说道：

"没有用，我做不到！"然后，乌龟把脑袋和四条腿缩进壳里，不再动弹。

AT this sudden commotion in their water, the fishes darted away and disappeared in a flash. But Twinkle didn't mind that, for all her interest was now centered in the struggling turtle.

She knelt upon the grass and bent over to watch it, and just then she thought she heard a small voice say:

"It's no use; I can't do it!" and then the turtle drew its head and legs between the shells and remained still.

"天哪！"唐可儿说，她完全被惊住了。随即她对着乌龟问道：

　　"刚才你说话了吗？"

　　没有回答。乌龟一动不动地躺着，好像死了一样。唐可儿心想，肯定是自己弄错了。于是，她捡起乌龟，托在手心里，重新走进小溪，慢慢地蹚着溪水，走回到她放鞋袜的地方。

"Good gracious!" said Twinkle, much astonished. Then, addressing the turtle, she asked:

"Did you say anything, a minute ago?"

There was no reply. The turtle lay as quiet as if it were dead. Twinkle thought she must have been mistaken; so she picked up the turtle and held it in the palm of her hand while she got into the water again and waded slowly back to where she had left her shoes and stockings.

唐可儿在观察乌龟
Twinkle Watching the Turtle

回到家，唐可儿把泥龟放在一个澡盆里。那是爸爸把一个木桶锯成两半做成的。然后，唐可儿往澡盆里倒了一些水，又在澡盆一侧的下面垫了块砖头，这样盆底高处有水，低处没有水，乌龟就可以根据自己的喜爱，或者待在水里，或者爬到澡盆垫高的、没有水的一头。唐可儿之所以这么做，是因为妈妈说过，乌龟有时喜欢待在水里，有时喜欢待在岸上。唐可儿的乌龟现在就可以自由选择了。

When she got home she put the mud-turtle in a tub which her papa had made by sawing a barrel in two. Then she put a little water into the tub and blocked it up by putting a brick under one side, so that the turtle could either stay in the water or crawl up the inclined bottom of the tub to where it was dry, whichever he pleased. She did this because mamma said that turtles sometimes liked to stay in the water and sometimes on land, and Twinkle's turtle could now take his choice.

澡盆的侧面很陡，乌龟没法爬上来逃走。小姑娘还体贴地把一些面包屑和碎肉放在乌龟够得到的地方，让它饿了的时候吃。

从那之后，唐可儿经常坐在那里观察乌龟，一坐就是好几个小时。乌龟在澡盆底部爬来爬去，在那个小水池里游泳，津津有味地吃放在它面前的食物，那样子别提多好玩了。

He couldn't climb up the steep sides of the tub and so get away, and the little girl thoughtfully placed crumbs of bread and fine bits of meat, where the turtle could get them whenever he felt hungry.

After that, Twinkle often sat for hours watching the turtle, which would crawl around the bottom of the tub, and swim in the little pool of water and eat the food placed before him in an eager and amusing way.

有时，唐可儿把它托在手里，仔细端详。这时候，泥龟就会伸出小脑袋，用一双亮晶晶的眼睛看着唐可儿，就跟小姑娘打量它时一样充满好奇。

唐可儿拥有这只乌龟正好一星期了。这天下午，唐可儿带了一些肉末来喂乌龟。她走到澡盆边，把乌龟抓起来。没想到，乌龟刚一探出脑袋，就对唐可儿说话了，声音很小，但很清楚：

At times she took him in her hand and examined him closely, and then the mud-turtle would put out its little head and look at her with its bright eyes as curiously as the girl looked at him.

She had owned her turtle just a week, when she came to the tub one afternoon and held him in her hand, intending to feed her pet some scraps of meat she had brought with her. But as soon as the turtle put out its head it said to her, in a small but distinct voice:

"早上好，唐可儿。"

唐可儿大吃一惊，手里的肉掉了，还差点儿把乌龟也扔了。但是她总算克制住自己的惊讶，用微微有点颤抖的声音问：

"你会说话？"

"没错，"乌龟回答，"但每过七天才说一次——当然啦，就是每个星期六。其他日子，我一句话也不会说。"

"Good morning, Twinkle."

She was so surprised that the meat dropped from her hand, and she nearly dropped the turtle, too. But she managed to control her astonishment, and asked, in a voice that trembled a little:

"Can you talk?"

"To be sure," replied the turtle; "but only on every seventh day—which of course is every Saturday. On other days I cannot talk at all."

"那么，我抓住你的时候，确实听见你说话了，是不是？"

"应该是吧。我被抓住时吃了一惊，没经考虑就开口说话了，那是一种坏习惯。可是在那之后，我打定主意不回答你的问话，因为那时候我对你尚不了解，担心把我的秘密透露给你不是明智之举。即使现在，我也必须请求你，千万别告诉任何人你有一只会说话的乌龟。"

"Then I really must have heard you speak when I caught you; didn't I?"

"I believe you did. I was so startled at being captured that I spoke before I thought, which is a bad habit to get into. But afterward I resolved not to answer when you questioned me, for I didn't know you then, and feared it would be unwise to trust you with my secret. Even now I must ask you not to tell any one that you have a turtle that knows how to talk."

"早上好，唐可儿"
"Good Morning, Twinkle"

第三章
Chapter III

乌龟讲述皱褶巨人的故事
The Turtle Tells of the Corrugated Giant

"啊，太奇妙了！"唐可儿兴奋地听着乌龟的话，说道。

"是啊，如果我是一只普通的乌龟，这确实很奇妙。"乌龟回答。

"难道你不是乌龟吗？"

"WHY, it's wonderful!" said Twinkle, who had listened eagerly to the turtle's speech.

"It would be wonderful, indeed, if I were but a simple turtle," was the reply.

"But aren't you a turtle?"

"当然，看我外表的样子，我就是一只再普通不过的小泥龟。"乌龟回答，"但是我想你会同意我的观点，皱褶巨人把我变成这样一种动物，算是很聪明了。"

"皱皱巨人（唐可儿一直说不好'皱褶巨人'这个词）是什么？"唐可儿问，好奇得透不过气来。

"Of course, so far as my outward appearance goes, I'm a common little mud-turtle," it answered; "and I think you will agree with me that it was rather clever in the Corrugated Giant to transform me into such a creature."

"What's a Corrulated Giant?" asked Twinkle, with breathless interest.

"皱褶巨人是一个巨怪，满身都是深深的皱纹，因为他身体里没有骨头支撑他的皮肉。"乌龟说，"我恨这个巨人，他恶毒而残酷，信不信由你。这个巨人对我同样也恨之入骨。所以，有一天我想去杀死他时，巨怪就把我变成了你面前这个无助的小动物。"

"那么，你变形之前是什么人呢？"小姑娘问。

"The Corrugated Giant is a monster that is full of deep wrinkles, because he has no bones inside him to hold his flesh up properly," said the turtle. "I hated this giant, who is both wicked and cruel, I assure you; and this giant hated me in return. So, when one day I tried to destroy him, the monster transformed me into the helpless little being you see before you."

"But who were you before you were transformed?" asked the girl.

"是仙境王子，名叫梅尔加，仙境的亮翅女王的第七个儿子。亮翅女王统治着这片土地北部的所有仙境。"

"你做乌龟多长时间了？"

"十四年，"乌龟深深叹了口气，回答道，"至少我认为是十四年。当然啦，在小溪里游来游去，在泥巴里找东西吃，使人很容易忘记时间。"

"A fairy prince named Melga, the seventh son of the fairy Queen Flutterlight, who rules all the fairies in the north part of this land."

"And how long have you been a turtle?"

"Fourteen years," replied the creature, with a deep sigh. "At least, I think it is fourteen years; but of course when one is swimming around in brooks and grubbing in the mud for food, one is apt to lose all track of time."

"确实是这样的。"唐可儿说，"这么说来，你年纪比我还大呢。"

"比你大多了，"乌龟说，"在皱褶巨人把我变成乌龟前，我就已经活了四百年。"

"那时候你头发变白了吗？"唐可儿问，"有白胡子吗？"

"I should think so, indeed," said Twinkle. "But, according to that, you're older than I am."

"Much older," declared the turtle. "I had lived about four hundred years before the Corrugated Giant turned me into a turtle."

"Was your head gray?" she asked; "and did you have white whiskers?"

亮翅女王

Queen Flutterlight

30

"当然没有！"乌龟说，"仙人的外表总是年轻美丽的，不管他们活了多少年。而且，仙人因为不会死，经常会活到很老很老。这是不用说的。"

"当然！"唐可儿赞同道，"妈妈跟我说过仙人的事。可是，你只能一直做一只泥龟吗？"

"那就看你愿不愿意帮助我了。"乌龟回答。

"No, indeed!" said the turtle. "Fairies are always young and beautiful in appearance, no matter how many years they have lived. And, as they never die, they're bound to get pretty old sometimes, as a matter of course."

"Of course!" agreed Twinkle. "Mama has told me about the fairies. But must you always be a mud-turtle?"

"That will depend on whether you are willing to help me or not," was the answer.

"哎呀，听起来真像书里的一个童话故事！"小姑娘喊道。

"是的，"乌龟说，"自从有了仙人之后，这些事情就一直在发生。说不定，你真会看到我们的一些冒险经历被写进书里呢。可是，你愿意帮助我吗？这是眼下最重要的问题。"

"我会尽我的全力。"唐可儿说。

"Why, it sounds just like a fairy tale in a book!" cried the little girl.

"Yes," replied the turtle, "these things have been happening ever since there were fairies, and you might expect some of our adventures would get into books. But are you willing to help me? That is the important thing just now."

"I'll do anything I can," said Twinkle.

"那么，"乌龟说，"我就可以期待在较短的时间内恢复原形了。但是你必须很勇敢，面对危险这样的小事不会退缩。"

听了这话，唐可儿的表情变得严肃了。

"但我肯定不希望受到伤害，"唐可儿说，"如果我出了什么事，爸爸妈妈准会崩退的（唐可儿口齿不清，把'崩溃'说成了'崩退'）。"

"Then," said the turtle, "I may expect to get back to my own form again in a reasonably short time. But you must be brave, and not shrink from such a little thing as danger."

That made Twinkle look solemn.

"Of course I don't want to get hurt," she said. "My mama and papa would go dis*truc*ted if anything happened to me."

"会发生一些事，这是不用说的，"乌龟声明道，"但只要你完全按照我的吩咐去做，就不会受到任何伤害。"

"我不用去跟那个皱巴巴巨人搏斗吧？"唐可儿不放心地问。

"不是皱巴巴巨人，是皱褶巨人。不用，你根本不用搏斗。当时机到来时，我会亲自作战。但是你必须跟我一起去黑山区，才能把我解救出来。"

"Something will happen, sure," declared the turtle; "but nothing that happens will hurt you in the least if you do exactly as I tell you."

"I won't have to fight that Carbolated Giant, will I?" Twinkle asked doubtfully.

"He isn't carbolated; he's corrugated. No, you won't have to fight at all. When the proper time comes I'll do the fighting myself. But you may have to come with me to the Black Mountains, in order to set me free."

"远吗？"唐可儿问。

"远，但我们去那儿不用花很长时间。"乌龟回答，"我会告诉你怎么做。只要你听从我的忠告，就不会有人知道你在跟仙人和冒险奇遇打交道。"

"还有皱纹巨人。"唐可儿补充道。

"Is it far?" she asked.

"Yes; but it won't take us long to go there," answered the turtle. "Now, I'll tell you what to do and, if you follow my advice no one will ever know you're been mixed up with fairies and strange adventures."

"And Collerated Giants," she added.

"是皱褶巨人。"乌龟纠正她，"这个星期六太晚了，来不及开始我们的旅程，只能再等一个星期。下个星期六早晨，你一大早吃过早饭就来找我，那时我会告诉你怎么做。"

"好的，"唐可儿说，"我不会忘记的。"

"另外，拜托你时不时地给我一点儿清水。我虽说是一只泥龟，但同时也是一位仙境的王子。实不相瞒，我更喜欢喝清水。"

"Corrugated," he corrected. "It is too late, this Saturday, to start upon our journey, so we must wait another week. But next Saturday morning do you come to me bright and early, as soon as you've had breakfast, and then I'll tell you what to do."

"All right," said Twinkle; "I won't forget."

"In the mean time, do give me a little clean water now and then. I'm a mud-turtle, sure enough; but I'm also a fairy prince, and I must say I prefer clean water."

乌龟解释它的计划

The Turtle Explains His Plans

"放心吧。"小姑娘保证道。

"好了，快把我放下，走吧，"乌龟继续说，"我要花整整一星期的时间来做计划，决定我们到底该怎么做。"

"I'll attend to it," promised the girl.

"Now put me down and run away," continued the turtle. "It will take me all the week to think over my plans, and decide exactly what we are to do."

第四章
Chapter IV

乌龟王子
还记得魔法
Prince Turtle
Remembers His Magic

唐可儿跟乌龟王子有了这次奇怪的谈话，之后的一星期都忐忑不安。每天一放学，唐可儿就跑到澡盆边，看乌龟是不是安然无恙——唐可儿担心它会以某种离奇的方式逃走或消失。在学校的时候，唐可儿很难集中精力上课，不止一次受到老师的批评。

TWINKLE was as nervous as she could be during all the week that followed this strange conversation with Prince Turtle. Every day, as soon as school was out, she would run to the tub to see if the turtle was still safe—for she worried lest it should run away or disappear in some strange manner. And during school hours it was such hard work to keep her mind on her lessons that teacher scolded her more than once.

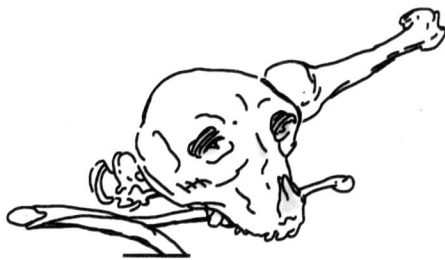

这个星期，被囚禁在乌龟身体里的仙境王子没有跟唐可儿说一句话，因为他要到星期六才能重新开口说话。因此，唐可儿为了表示对王子的关注，只能尽量给他提供最精美的食物和大量干净的清水。

最后，唐可儿冒险的那一天到来了，她刚从早饭桌上离开，就出来奔向了澡盆。她的仙人乌龟依然在那儿。

The fairy imprisoned in the turtle's form had nothing to say to her during this week, because he would not be allowed to talk again until Saturday; so the most that Twinkle could do to show her interest in the Prince was to give him the choicest food she could get and supply him with plenty of fresh, clean water.

At last the day of her adventure arrived, and as soon as she could get away from the breakfast table Twinkle ran out to the tub.

唐可儿趴在澡盆上时，乌龟探出脑袋，用尖尖细细的嗓音喊道："早上好！"

　　"早上好。"唐可儿回答。

　　"你仍然愿意帮助我吗？"乌龟问。

　　"当然。"唐可儿说。

　　"那就把我放在你手里吧。"乌龟说。

There was her fairy turtle, safe as could be, and as she leaned over the tub he put out his head and called "Good morning!" in his small, shrill voice.

"Good morning," she replied.

"Are you still willing and ready to assist me?" asked the turtle.

"To be sure," said Twinkle.

"Then take me in your hand," said he.

穿越天空的旅程

The Trip Through the Air

44

于是，唐可儿把乌龟从澡盆里拿出来，托在手心。这时，乌龟说道：

"现在请密切注意，完全按我说的去做，就会一切顺利。首先，我们要去黑山区。所以，你必须跟着我重复这句话：'乌勒，阿勒，依勒，噢勒！'"

"乌勒，阿勒，依勒，噢勒！"唐可儿说。

So she picked him out of the tub and placed him upon her hand. And the turtle said:

"Now pay strict attention, and do exactly as I tell you, and all will be well. In the first place, we want to get to the Black Mountains; so you must repeat after me these words: 'Uller; aller; iller; oller!' "

"Uller; aller; iller; oller!" said Twinkle.

顿时，一股狂风席卷而来。风真大啊，吹得唐可儿的眼睛什么也看不见。于是，唐可儿用一只胳膊挡住脸，另一只手紧紧抓着乌龟。她的裙子扑啦啦地摆动，似乎要从她身体上撕扯开去，而那顶太阳帽没有系紧，一眨眼就被吹得没影儿了。

幸好，持续的时间不长。过了一会儿，风停了，唐可儿发现自己又能呼吸了。

The next minute it seemed as though a gale of wind had struck her. It blew so strongly against her eyes that she could not see; so she covered her face with one arm while with the other hand she held fast to the turtle. Her skirts fluttered so wildly that it seemed as if they would tear themselves from her body, and her sun-bonnet, not being properly fastened, was gone in a minute.

But it didn't last long, fortunately. After a few moments the wind stopped, and she found she could breathe again.

她看看周围，突然倒吸了一口冷气：她不是在自己家的后院，而是站在一座美丽的山坡上，面前是她从未见过的最翠绿诱人的山谷。

　　"好了，我们到了。"乌龟说。从声音听，它感到很高兴。"我就知道我并没有忘记我的仙人智慧。"

　　"我们是在哪儿呢？"小姑娘问。

Then she looked around her and drew another long breath, for instead of being in the back yard at home she stood on the side of a beautiful mountain, and spread before her were the loveliest green valleys she had ever beheld.

"Well, we're here," said the turtle, in a voice that sounded as if he were well pleased. "I thought I hadn't forgotten my fairy wisdom."

"Where are we?" asked the child.

"当然是在黑山区。"乌龟回答，"这一路可不近，但我们没用多长时间就到了，是不是？"

"确实是。"唐可儿回答，仍然顺着山坡凝望山谷里鲜花盛开的草地。

"In the Black Mountains, of course," was the reply. "We've come a good way, but it didn't take us long to arrive, did it?"

"No, indeed," she answered, still gazing down the mountain side at the flower-strewn grass-land of the valleys.

"这儿，"乌龟把它的小脑袋尽量伸得很长，说道，"就是仙境之国，是我以前生活的地方。你能看见远处那些美丽的宫殿吗？亮翅女王和我们的臣民就住在那里。在你的左边，矗立在山坡上的那座阴森森的城堡，就是皱褶巨人住的地方。"

"我什么也看不见！"唐可儿喊道，"我只看见山谷、鲜花和草地。"

"This," said the turtle, sticking his little head out of the shell as far as it would go, "is the realm of the fairies, where I used to dwell. Those beautiful palaces you see yonder are inhabited by Queen Flutterlight and my people, and that grim castle at your left, standing on the side of the mountain, is where the Corrugated Giant lives."

"I don't see anything! " exclaimed Twinkle; "that is, nothing but the valleys and the flowers and grass. "

"用它擦擦你的眼皮"
"Rub Your Eyelids With It"

"是啊，我忘记了，你们凡人的眼睛是看不见这些东西的。但是，你若要把我从这可怕的形态中解救出去，让我恢复原形，就必须把一切都看得清清楚楚。好吧，把我放在地上，因为我必须寻找一种特殊植物，它的叶子具有神奇的功效。"

"True; I had forgotten that these things are invisible to your mortal eyes. But it is necessary that you should see all clearly, if you are going to rescue me from this terrible form and restore me to my natural shape. Now, put me down upon the ground, for I must search for a particular plant whose leaf has a magic virtue."

于是，唐可儿把小乌龟放下，小乌龟开始在地上跑来跑去，仔细地查看山坡上草丛里的各种不同植物。可是，它的腿太短了，乌龟壳又那么重，没法走得很快。不一会儿，它就叫唐可儿再把它拿起来，托着它靠近地面，在那些植物间行走。唐可儿这么做了，她感觉搜寻了很长时间，乌龟突然叫道：

So Twinkle put him down, and the little turtle began running around here and there, looking carefully at the different plants that grew amongst the grass on the mountain side. But his legs were so short and his shell-covered body so heavy, that he couldn't move very fast; so presently he called for her to pick him up again, and hold him close to the ground while she walked among the plants. She did this, and after what seemed a long search the turtle suddenly cried out:

"停！找到了！这就是我想要的植物。"

"哪棵——这棵？"小姑娘碰了碰一片宽宽的绿叶，问道。

"是的。把叶子从茎上拔下来，用它擦擦你的眼皮。"

唐可儿照办了，用叶子把眼皮好好擦了几下。当她再睁开眼睛时，就看见了真正的仙境之国。

"Stop! Here it is! This is the plant I want."

"Which—this?" asked the girl, touching a broad green leaf.

"Yes. Pluck the leaf from the stem and rub your eyelids with it."

She obeyed, and having rubbed her lids well with the leaf, she again opened her eyes and beheld the real Fairyland.

第五章
Chapter V

唐可儿
保证会勇敢
Twinkle Promises to Be Brave

在山谷的中央，有一大片宫殿，看上去像是用水晶、银子、珍珠母和金箔建成的。这些童话般的建筑真是说不出的典雅和美丽。唐可儿毫不犹豫就相信了她眼前所见的确实是仙境之国。尽管站在这么远的山坡上，她也仿佛能看见那些轻灵的仙人，张着薄薄的翅膀，在漂亮的宫殿间轻盈地飞翔，在铺满宝石的街道上优雅地穿行。

IN the center of the valley was a great cluster of palaces that appeared to be built of crystal and silver and mother-of-pearl, and golden filigree-work. So dainty and beautiful were these fairy dwellings that Twinkle had no doubt for an instant but that she gazed upon fairyland. She could almost see, from the far mountain upon which she stood, the airy, gauze-winged forms of the fairies themselves, floating gently amidst their pretty palaces and moving gracefully along the jeweled streets.

"那道栅栏是有魔法的"
"That Fence is Enchanted"

可是，另一番景象吸引了她的注意——一座灰暗、丑陋的大城堡，阴森森地矗立在她左边的山坡上。它俯瞰着美丽可爱的宫殿之城，就像一团乌云笼罩着蔚蓝的天际。小姑娘一看见它，就忍不住打了个寒噤。这座城堡周围都是带着铁尖的高高的栅栏。

But another sight now attracted her attention—a big, gray, ugly looking castle standing frowning on the mountain side at her left. It overlooked the lovely city of palaces like a dark cloud on the edge of a blue sky, and the girl could not help giving a shudder as she saw it. All around the castle was a high fence of iron spikes.

"那道栅栏是有魔法的，"乌龟说，它似乎知道唐可儿正看着城堡，"没有任何仙人能够越过，因为巨人拥有阻止仙人通过的法力。但是巨人从来没有禁止凡人通过那道栅栏，因为谁也不曾想到会有一个凡人能够来到这里，或能够看见城堡。所以，我才把你带到这个地方。所以，只有你才能帮助我。"

　　"That fence is enchanted," said the turtle, as if he knew she was looking at it; "and no fairy can pass it, because the power to prevent it has been given to the giant. But a mortal has never been forbidden to pass the fence, for no one ever supposed that a mortal would come here or be able to see it. That is the reason I have brought you to this place, and the reason why you alone are able to help me."

"天哪！"唐可儿惊呼道，"我必须面对老皱巨人吗？"

"是皱褶巨人。"乌龟说。

"我知道他肯定特别可怕，"唐可儿哀叫，"他的名字就这么难念。"

"你必须要面对他，"乌龟大声说，"但是不用害怕，我会保护你不受任何伤害。"

"Gracious!" cried Twinkle; "must I meet the Carbonated Giant?"

"He's corrugated," said the turtle.

"I know he's something dreadful," she wailed, "because he's so hard to pronounce."

"You will surely have to meet him," declared the turtle; "but do not fear, I will protect you from all harm."

"可是，皱胖巨人是一个那么大的大家伙，"小姑娘将信将疑地说，"一只泥龟肯定不是他的对手。我想我还是回家吧。"

"那不可能，"乌龟说道，"你离家太远，没有我的帮助，你不可能回去。所以，你还是乖乖地听我吩咐吧。"

"我需要做什么？"唐可儿问。

"Well, a Corralated Giant's a mighty big person," said the girl, doubtfully, "and a mud-turtle isn't much of a fighter. I guess I'll go home."

"That is impossible," declared the turtle. "You are too far from home ever to get back without my help, so you may as well be good and obedient."

"What must I do?" she asked.

"我们等到快中午的时候，巨人就会把锅放在炉子上煮午饭。看到他的烟囱里冒出烟来，我们就知道时候到了。然后，你必须迈开大步走向城堡，走进巨人干活的厨房，麻利地把我扔进滚开的锅里。你需要做的事就这么多。"

"我绝对做不到！"唐可儿一口咬定。

"We will wait until it is nearly noon, when the giant will put his pot on the fire to boil his dinner. We can tell the right time by watching the smoke come out of his chimney. Then you must march straight up to the castle and into the kitchen where the giant is at work, and throw me quickly into the boiling kettle. That is all that you will be required to do."

"I never could do it!" declared Twinkle.

寻找具有神奇功效的鲜花

Hunting the Magic Flower

"为什么？"

"你会被烫死的，然后我就成了杀人犯！"

"胡说！"乌龟气恼地说，"我知道自己在做什么。只要你按我说的去做，我就只会被烫那么一下，接着便会恢复我的原形。记住，我是个仙人，仙人是不会像你想的那么容易被烫死的。"

"Why not?"

"You'd be scalded to death, and then I'd be a murderer!"

"Nonsense!" said the turtle, peevishly. "I know what I'm doing, and if you obey me I'll not be scalded but an instant; for then I'll resume my own form. Remember that I'm a fairy, and fairies can't be killed so easily as you seem to think."

"不会烫疼你吗？"唐可儿问。

"只会疼一下。但是报偿那么丰厚，我不会在乎这一眨眼的疼痛。你愿意为我做这件事吗？"

"我会尽力的。"唐可儿一脸严肃地回答。

"那我将会十分感激，"乌龟王子说，"并保证事成后把你平安送回家，速度跟你来的时候一样快。"

"Won't it hurt you?" she inquired.

"Only for a moment; but the reward will be so great that I won't mind an instant's pain. Will you do this favor for me?"

"I'll try, " replied Twinkle, gravely.

"Then I will be very grateful," said Prince Turtle, "and agree to afterward send you home safe and sound, and as quickly as you came."

第六章
Chapter VI

唐可儿
遇见皱褶巨人
Twinkle Meets the Corrugated Giant

"现在，趁我们等待的时候，"仙人乌龟继续说道，"我想找一种具有神奇功效的鲜花。它能保护凡人不受伤害。倒不是担心我不能照顾你，只是为了保险起见，以防万一。"

"那就更好了。"唐可儿热切地说，"那种花在哪儿？"

"我们去找找。"乌龟回答。

"AND now, while we are waiting," continued the fairy turtle, "I want to find a certain flower that has wonderful powers to protect mortals from any injury. Not that I fear I shall be unable to take care of you, but it's just as well to be on the safe side."

"Better," said Twinkle, earnestly. "Where's the flower?"

"We'll hunt for it," replied the turtle.

于是，小姑娘把乌龟托在手里，让它能看到地上所有的鲜花。她开始在山坡上走来走去，周围的一切都是这么美丽。要不是眼前那座灰色城堡不断提醒小姑娘，使她想到必须面对住在城堡里的可怕巨人，她本来是会感到非常满足和快乐的。

So holding him in her hand in such a way that he could see all the flowers that grew, the girl began wandering over the mountain side, and everything was so beautiful around her that she would have been quite contented and happy had not the gray castle been before her to remind her constantly that she must face the terrible giant who lived within it.

那种鲜花终于找到了——一种漂亮的粉红色的花，看上去像双瓣雏菊，但肯定不是雏菊，因为我从来没听说过雏菊具有什么神奇功效。鲜花找到后，乌龟叫唐可儿把花摘下来，牢牢地别在衣服前面，唐可儿照办了。

They found the flower at last—a pretty pink blossom that looked like a double daisy, but must have been something else, because a daisy has no magic power that I ever heard of. And when it was found, the turtle told her to pick the flower and pin it fast to the front of her dress; which she did.

唐可儿成功挤过栅栏
Twinkle Manages to Squeeze Through

就在这时，巨人的烟囱里开始冒出大股大股的黑烟。仙人乌龟说，巨人一定是在做饭，等他们赶到城堡时，锅里肯定就煮开了。

想到要接近巨人的堡垒，唐可儿还是不禁有点儿害怕，但她努力让自己勇敢起来。于是，她迈着轻快的脚步往前走，最后来到了那道有着铁尖的栅栏前。

By that time the smoke began to roll out of the giant's chimney in big black clouds; so the fairy turtle said the giant must be getting dinner, and the pot would surely be boiling by the time they got to the castle.

Twinkle couldn't help being a little afraid to approach the giant's stronghold, but she tried to be brave, and so stepped along briskly until she came to the fence of iron spikes.

"你必须从两根铁栅栏之间挤过去。"乌龟说。

唐可儿认为这简直不可能。然而，令她惊讶的是，这竟然非常容易，她不费劲就挤过了栅栏，连裙子都没有刮破。然后，她顺着一条宽宽的道路走上去，路两边堆积着许多白森森的羊骨头，这些羊都是被巨人吃掉的。唐可儿一直走到城堡的大门口，门微微开着条缝。

"You must squeeze through between two of the spikes," said the turtle.

She didn't think it could possibly be done; but to her surprise it was quite easy, and she managed to squeeze through the fence without even tearing her dress. Then she walked up a great driveway, which was lined with white skulls of many sheep which the giant had eaten, to the front door of the castle, which stood ajar.

"进去吧。"乌龟说。唐可儿就大着胆子进了门，穿过一个拱顶高高的大厅，朝后面一个房间走去。

"这就是厨房。"乌龟说，"快进去吧，直接走到锅前，把我扔进滚开的水里。"

唐可儿进去的速度倒是很快，可是她突然站住，发出一声惊愕的喊叫，因为她面前就站着那个丑陋的巨人，正在用一只巨大的风箱吹火。

"Go in," said the turtle; so she boldly entered and passed down a high arched hall toward a room in the rear.

"This is the kitchen," said the turtle, "Enter quickly, go straight to the kettle, and throw me into the boiling water."

Twinkle entered quickly enough, but then she stopped short with a cry of amazement; for there before her stood the ugly giant, blowing the fire with an immense pair of bellows.

泥龟王子变成
梅尔加王子

Prince Mud-Turtle
Becomes Prince Melga

巨人大约有十个男人那么大，有两个男人那么高。可是，因为没有骨头，他看上去是肉堆起来的，皮肤全都像手风琴或老式相机一样布满皱褶，就连他的脸也皱巴巴的，鼻子从两道肉褶儿中间戳出来，眼睛也挤在两道肉褶儿中间。厨房的一头就是那个大壁炉，上面挂着一个铁锅，里面有一把大铁勺。厨房的另一头是一张餐桌，上面已经摆好了餐具。

THE giant was as big around as ten men, and as tall as two; but, having no bones, he seemed pushed together, so that his skin wrinkled up like the sides of an accordeon, or a photograph camera, even his face being so wrinkled that his nose stuck out between two folds of flesh and his eyes from between two more. In one end of the kitchen was the great fireplace, above which hung an iron kettle with a big iron spoon in it. And at the other end was a table set for dinner.

唐可儿遇见皱褶巨人

Twinkle Meets the Corrugated Giant

因为巨人挡在了铁锅和唐可儿之间，唐可儿没法按照乌龟吩咐的那样把它扔进锅里。于是，她迟疑了，不知道怎么听从仙人的指示。就在这时，巨人正好转过身来，看见了她。

　　"天哪，老伽玛的胡子啊——老伽玛是我的一个老祖宗，被巨人杀手杰克杀死了！"巨人喊道。对于这么大块头的人来说，他的声音倒是非常温和，"我们面前的这是谁呀？"

As the giant was standing between the kettle and Twinkle, she could not do as the turtle had commanded, and throw him into the pot. So she hesitated, wondering how to obey the fairy. Just then the giant happened to turn around and see her.

"By the whiskers of Gammarog—who was one of my ancestors that was killed by Jack the Giant-Killer!" he cried, but in a very mild voice for so big a person. "Whom have we here?"

"我是唐可儿。"小姑娘说着，深深吸了口气。

"那么，为了惩罚你擅自闯进我城堡的胡闹行为，我要把你变成我的奴隶。如果哪一天你干活不卖力，我就把你拿去喂我那条长有十七个脑袋的狗。我自己从来不吃小姑娘。我爱吃羊肉。"

唐可儿听到这些可怕的话，心脏几乎都停止了跳动。

"I'm Twinkle," said the girl, drawing a long breath.

"Then, to pay you for your folly in entering my castle, I will make you my slave, and some day, if you're not good, I'll feed you to my seventeen-headed dog. I never eat little girls myself. I prefer mutton."

Twinkle's heart almost stopped beating when she heard these awful words.

她只能一动不动地站在那儿，用哀求的眼光看着巨人。可是，她把仙人泥龟紧紧地握在手里，不让巨人看见。

"喂，你瞪着眼睛看什么呢？"皱褶巨人气呼呼地喊道，"赶快给我吹火，奴隶！"

巨人站到一旁，让唐可儿过去，于是唐可儿立刻朝壁炉跑去。铁锅就在她眼前了，一伸手就能够到，锅里的水咕嘟咕嘟沸腾着。

All she could do was to stand still and look imploringly at the giant. But she held the fairy mud-turtle clasped tight in her hand, so that the monster couldn't see it.

"Well, what are you staring at?" shouted the Corrugated Giant, angrily. "Blow up that fire this instant, slave!"

He stood aside for her to pass, and Twinkle ran at once to the fireplace. The pot was now before her, and within easy reach, and it was bubbling hot.

说时迟那时快，唐可儿手一扬，把乌龟扔进了沸水中。接着，她被自己的行为吓得尖叫一声，赶忙往后一退，看会发生什么情况。

　　别忘了乌龟是个仙人啊，它非常清楚怎样最有效地破除敌人对它施的魔法。唐可儿刚把它扔进沸水，就听见一阵儿很响的嘶嘶声，大团的蒸汽弥漫开来，一时间遮住了壁炉。

In an instant she reached out her hand and tossed the turtle into the boiling water; and then, with a cry of horror at her own action, she drew back to see what would happen.

The turtle was a fairy, all right; and he had known very well the best way to break the enchantment his enemy had put upon him. For no sooner had Twinkle tossed him into the boiling pot than a great hissing was heard, and a cloud of steam hid for an instant the fireplace.

王子亲吻唐可儿的手
The Prince Kisses Twinkle's Hand

然后，蒸汽散开，一位英俊的年轻王子走了出来，全副武装。乌龟又变回了仙人，铁锅变成了一个结实的盾牌，戴在王子的左臂上，铁勺此刻变成了一把闪闪发亮的长剑。

Then, as it cleared away, a handsome young prince stepped forward, fully armed; for the turtle was again a fairy, and the kettle had changed into a strong shield which he bore upon his left arm, and the iron spoon was now a long and glittering sword.

唐可儿
得到一枚奖章

Twinkle
Receives a Medal

看见梅尔加王子站在自己面前，巨人发出一声小公牛般的咆哮，转眼间就抓起放在旁边的一根大棒，把它抡过了头顶。可是，没等大棒落下来，王子就冲向巨人，把宝剑扎进了巨人布满皱褶的身体，扎得很深很深。巨怪又发出一声咆哮，想要反击，可是宝剑严重刺伤了他，而且王子一次又一次地把剑扎向恶毒的怪物。最后，这个布满皱褶的敌人终于翻滚在地上，死了。

THE giant gave a roar like that of a baby bull when he saw Prince Melga standing before him, and in a twinkling he had caught up a big club that stood near and began whirling it over his head. But before it could descend, the prince ran at him and stuck his sword as far as it would go into the corrugated body of the giant. Again the monster roared and tried to fight; but the sword had hurt him badly, and the prince pushed it into the evil creature again and again, until the end came, and his corrugated enemy rolled over upon the floor quite dead.

这时，仙人转向唐可儿，然后跪在唐可儿面前，吻她的手。

"非常感谢你解救了我。"王子用悦耳的声音说，"你是一位非常勇敢的小姑娘！"

"这我可不敢肯定，"唐可儿回答，"当时我吓得魂都没了！"

Then the fairy turned to Twinkle, and kneeling before her he kissed her hand.

"Thank you very much," he said, in a sweet voice, "for setting me free. You are a very brave little girl!"

"I'm not so sure about that," she answered. "I was dreadfully scared!"

王子牵起唐可儿的手，领着她走出了城堡。唐可儿不用再挤过那道栅栏了，因为仙子只要念一句咒语，大门就一下子敞开了。当他们转身回望时，皱褶巨人的城堡以及城堡里所有的一切，统统都消失了，无论凡人还是仙人的眼睛都再也不会看见。每当有巨人死去，准会发生这样的事情。

Now he took her hand and led her from the castle; and she didn't have to squeeze through the fence again, because the fairy had only to utter a magic word and the gate flew open. And when they turned to look back, the castle of the Corrugated Giant, with all that it had contained, had vanished from sight, never to be seen again by either mortal or fairy eyes. For that was sure to happen whenever the giant was dead.

"不要忘记我，唐可儿"

"Don't Forget Me, Twinkle"

88

王子领着唐可儿来到仙境宫殿所在的山谷，臣民们都围过来欢迎王子。王子告诉他们，这个小姑娘对他多么好，是小姑娘的勇气帮助他打败了巨人，恢复了自己的原形。所有的仙子都用好话称赞唐可儿。美丽的亮翅女王，看上去那么年轻，简直不可能是英俊王子的母亲。她送给小姑娘一枚金质奖章，上面刻着一只小小的泥龟。

The prince led Twinkle into the valley where the fairy palaces stood, and told all his people, when they crowded around to welcome him, how kind the little girl had been to him, and how her courage had enabled him to defeat the giant and to regain his proper form. And all the fairies praised Twinkle with kind words, and the lovely Queen Flutterlight, who seemed altogether too young to be the mother of the handsome prince, gave to the child a golden medal with a tiny mud-turtle engraved upon one side of it.

他们准备了精美的盛宴，小姑娘尽情地吃了仙境的许多糖果蜜饯。然后，她对梅尔加王子说，她想回家了。

"好吧。"王子说，"不要忘记我，唐可儿，虽然我们可能永远不会再见面了。我会把你送回家，速度跟你来的时候一样快。但是你的眼睛已经用神奇的麦塔叶擦过，肯定一直会看见许多奇异的景象，那是其他凡人看不见的。"

Then, after a fine feast had been prepared, and the little girl had eaten all she could of the fairy sweetmeats, she told Prince Melga she would like to go home again.

"Very well, " said he. "Don't forget me, Twinkle, although we probably shall never meet again. I'll send you home quite as safely as you came; but as your eyes have been rubbed with the magic maita-leaf, you will doubtless always see many strange sights that are hidden from other mortals. "

"没关系。"唐可儿说。

然后，她告别了那些仙人，王子念了一句咒语。又是一阵狂风刮来。狂风过后，唐可儿发现自己又回到了自家的后院。

她坐在草地上，揉揉眼睛，为自己奇异的冒险经历惊叹不已。这时，妈妈来到后门廊上，说道：

"I don't mind," said Twinkle.

Then she bade good-bye to the fairies, and the prince spoke a magic word. There was another rush of wind, and when it had passed Twinkle found herself once more in the back yard at home.

As she sat upon the grass rubbing her eyes and wondering at the strange adventure that had befallen her, mamma came out upon the back porch and said:

"你的乌龟从澡盆里爬出来，逃走了。"

"是啊，"唐可儿说，"我知道。我很高兴这样！"

她把秘密藏在了自己心里。

"Your turtle has crawled out of the tub and run away."

"Yes," said Twinkle, "I know; and I'm glad of it!"

But she kept her secret to herself.

图书在版编目（CIP）数据

解救泥龟王子：汉英对照/（美）莱曼·弗兰克·鲍姆著；马爱农译.
北京：中国国际广播出版社，2016.11
（唐可儿奇遇记）
ISBN 978-7-5078-3901-2

Ⅰ.①解…　Ⅱ.①莱…②马…　Ⅲ.①英语—儿童读物　Ⅳ.①H319.4

中国版本图书馆CIP数据核字（2016）第241528号

唐可儿奇遇记：解救泥龟王子

著　　者	［美］莱曼·弗兰克·鲍姆
译　　者	马爱农
责任编辑	林钰鑫　李　卉
版式设计	国广设计室
责任校对	徐秀英

出版发行	中国国际广播出版社［010-83139469　010-83139489（传真）］
社　　址	北京市西城区天宁寺前街2号北院A座一层
	邮编：100055
网　　址	www.chirp.com.cn
经　　销	新华书店
印　　刷	北京艺堂印刷有限公司

开　　本	650×950　1/16
字　　数	80千字
印　　张	7
版　　次	2016年11月　北京第一版
印　　次	2016年11月　第一次印刷
定　　价	42.00元（含mp3光盘）

唐可儿奇遇记

出品人：宇清
策　　划：李卉
责任编辑：林钰鑫　李卉
装帧设计：Guangfu Design / 张晖
音乐合成：侯英珊